CONTENTS

Watch out for the *Sign of the Foot*! Whenever you see this sign in the book it means there are some more details at the *FOOT* of the page. Like here.

BEFORE IT BEGINS

ALL'S QUIET

Once upon a time there was a mighty continent. Its name was Europe and the year was 1914. It was at peace:

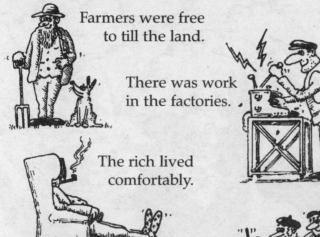

Farmers were free to till the land.

There was work in the factories.

The rich lived comfortably.

Artists painted and musicians played beautiful music.

Scientists discovered new wonders.

Then something horrible happened ...

WAR!

The mighty continent was torn apart by a terrible war. The most terrible war there had ever been - over nine million soldiers died. Before the war these same soldiers had been the farmers, the workers, the scientists and the musicians who had lived peacefully in the mighty continent. After it was over, their bodies, if laid head to toe, would have stretched for 15,084

kilometres (9,375 miles) - nearly half way around the world. A generation of young men was slaughtered.

This terrible war was called the Great War because there'd never been another war like it. Later, after a second terrible war twenty-one years later, the Great War became known as World War I and the new war was called World War II.

WHO, WHEN, WHERE - AND WHY?

WHO:

The war was fought between two groups of countries. On one side were the *Allies* 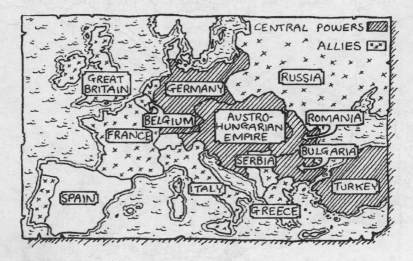, including Britain, France and Russia, and on the other side were the *Central Powers*, including Germany, the Austro-Hungarian Empire and Turkey. Towards the end of the war the USA joined the Allies.

The Allies won and the Central Powers lost.

WHEN:

World War I started in the summer of 1914 and finished in November 1918. It had four stages:

1 1914 *'It'll be over by Christmas'*. At this stage most people thought it would be a short war.

2 1915 *'Stuck in the mud'*. Nobody won and nobody lost. Armies got bogged down where they were.

If two or more countries agree to fight together in time of war they are called *allies*.

8

3 1916-17 '*Slaughter*'. Generals spent the lives of their men by the million trying to clamber out of the mud.

4 1917-18 '*The end game*'. Russia stopped fighting due to a revolution, the USA joined in and tanks were used in battle. The Central Powers crumbled.

WHERE:

Most of the fighting was in Europe, along a line from the English Channel to Switzerland, also in eastern Europe. There was some fighting in the Middle East and Africa as well.

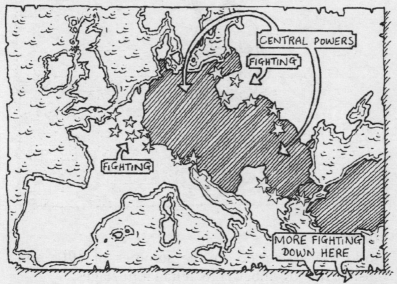

WHY:

In 1914 the rulers of Germany told themselves that Germany was in danger of attack by her neighbours. So they decided to attack first.

Their plan was to win a quick war against France in the west, followed by another quick war against Russia in the east. They seized an excuse and started fighting.

The Germans took a huge risk and it went horribly wrong. The quick war turned into a long slogging match against a more powerful enemy, which, if the truth be told, the Germans never really had much chance of winning.

As they were about to find out ...

PARADISE LOST

THE WORLD BEFORE THE WAR

Once the war had started, soldiers looked back on the world before the war as if it had been some sort of paradise. That paradise was a more simple place than the world we know today. Before 1914 many of the gadgets and gizmos that we take for granted had been invented but they were too expensive for most people.

THINGS PEOPLE *DIDN'T* HAVE IN 1914

Aeroplanes (All right, so most people  don't own aeroplanes even nowadays, but at least we get to fly in them.)

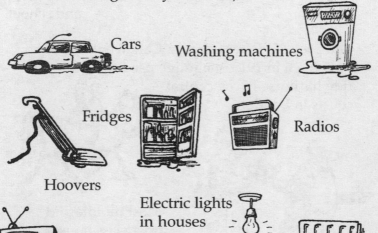

Cars

Washing machines

Fridges

Radios

Hoovers

Electric lights in houses

Televisions (not invented yet)

Central-heating

Things people *did* have in 1914

In 1914 there had been no major war in Europe for over forty years. The world was a quieter and more peaceful place than it is today. Life was good and getting better - for the rich and the middle classes anyway.

Even in Britain, then the most industrialised country in the world, the countryside was beautiful with lots of hedges and small fields.

Many people still worked on the land. Gentle winding lanes connected the villages and each village was a world of its own, with its own shops and school.

The pace of life was slower. Cars were rare. Even in 1913 one judge used to ride his horse to the central courts in London.

Most middle and upper class houses had servants to do the housework.

POSH PEOPLE'S POLITE PARADISE

Before the First World War, life was much stricter in many ways than it is today, even for the upper classes. There were more unwritten rules about how you should and shouldn't behave:

You weren't meant to talk to people unless you'd been introduced to them first.

 It was strictly against the rules for unmarried men and women to be alone together.

Women rode horses 'side saddle'. Their long skirts stopped them from dangling their legs on either side of the horse. It was almost unheard of for women to wear trousers, although a few wore 'bloomers' for cycling.

 Posh (and not so posh) women had special 'at home' days when visitors called.

Almost everyone went to church on Sundays.

 When a man visited, he carried his hat, gloves and stick into the drawing (living) room. It was thought rude to leave them in the hall.

Not so posh - and not quite paradise ...

Of course this world of servants and 'at home' days wasn't a paradise for everyone - not for the servants at any rate:

Most working people worked a full six day week and there were no paid holidays - except for servants, funnily enough.

Living conditions were often unhealthy and overcrowded.

Food was poor and, due to their bad diet, poor people tended to grow up much shorter than richer people. When the war came, the soldiers, who came from poorer families, were usually much shorter than their officers, who came from richer families.

A good education was very hard to come by unless you had money.

TOP DOG SNOBS

In 1914 each of the countries of Europe was ruled by a small group of 'top' people. The top people had money and power.

 *Germany* was ruled by the Kaiser (Emperor) and his chief minister, the Chancellor. They were helped by the *junkers* (landed nobles), the generals and some big business men.

 Britain was mainly ruled by a small group of top families through the Houses of Parliament. Britain was extremely rich and had a huge empire - it owned and controlled many other countries - so the top people were very rich indeed.

One of the problems with the world in 1914 was that nearly everyone thought their own country was better than anyone else's. Such ideas are dangerous - as World War I proved.

I'm a British lord. Britain is the richest country in the world and has the largest empire, so I'm better than anyone else.

I'm a German junker (noble). Britain is on the way out. Germany will soon be the most important country in the world, so I'm better than anyone else.

I'm a Russian lord. Russia is a huge, powerful country with a population almost equal to all the rest of Europe put together, so I'm better than anyone else.

I'm a French business man. France is the most civilized country in Europe and has a huge empire, so I'm better than anyone else.

I'm an American business man. I'm well away from any trouble and I'm getting richer by the minute, so I'm better than anyone else.

In fact, the pre-war world may have *seemed* like paradise to the soldiers who looked back on it from the horror of war, but this paradise wasn't ruled by angels at all. If any real angels were watching, they must have been worried ...

UNDER STARTER'S ORDERS

HOW IT BEGAN

THE BLACK HAND GANG

On 28 June 1914, Archduke Franz Ferdinand, the heir to the throne of the Austrian Empire 🐾 was visiting Bosnia, with his wife. Bosnia was a small country which had been swallowed up by the Austrian Empire only six years earlier.

> The majority of Bosnians were actually Serbs who wanted independence from Austria and to join up with next-door Serbia. Some Bosnian Serbs joined the Black Hand Gang, a secret society dedicated to winning freedon for Serbs everywhere.

Also in Bosnia was a young Serbian student called Gavrilo Princip, probably a member of the Black Hand Gang and certainly a member of 'Young Bosnia', another anti-Austrian movement. Gavrilo shot dead the Archduke and

---

 The full name of the Austrian Empire was the *Austro-Hungarian* Empire because it included Hungary.

his wife in broad daylight in front of a horrified crowd in the centre of Sarajevo, the Bosnian capital - and started the First World War.

BASKET CASE

The Austrian Empire was a basket case - a basket of different countries and peoples - and most of them wanted to get out of the basket as soon as possible.

Back in Vienna, the capital of the Austrian Empire, old Emperor Franz Josef was soon swamped with letters from all the leaders of Europe. They said how sorry they were about the murder of the Archduke, his nephew. Josef wrote back and thanked them politely (even though he couldn't stand his nephew). There was more at stake than a family quarrel.

If Austria was seen to give way to mad Serbs like Gavrilo Princip and allowed Serbs to break away from the Empire, several other countries might try to break away as well. The Serbs must be punished as an example. That was why on 28 July 1914, Austria declared war on Serbia.

FRIENDS

Franz Josef felt that Austria was strong enough to go to war because Germany had promised to back him up. Germany was a big, powerful country. But even so, Austria were taking a huge risk ...

Would the Russians come to the aid of their friends the Serbs?

Would the French come to the aid of their friends the Russians?

Would the British come to the aid of the French?

Oh well, the Austrians went ahead anyway.

NOT VERY GOOD KNITTING

In 1914 all the big European countries were tied up in two great 'alliances'. (Groups of allies, see page 8.) The 'allies' had promised to defend each other in case of attack on one of their members. This meant that if any two countries from different alliances started fighting,

BRITAIN: POPULATION 45 MILLION, POWERFUL NAVY BUT A SMALL ARMY OF ONLY 250,000 SOLDIERS.

GERMANY: POPULATION 70 MILLION, AN ARMY OF 850,000 SOLDIERS

FRANCE: POPULATION 35 MILLION, AN ARMY OF 700,000 SOLDIERS

ITALY: POPULATION 35 MILLION

Central Powers in 1914
Joined the Central Powers soon after

all the rest were pretty well bound to be drawn in. Europe was tied up like a piece of knitting. Once it started to unravel, nothing could stop it.

RUSSIA: A VAST POPULATION, AND AN ARMY OF AROUND 1 MILLION SOLDIERS

AUSTRO-HUNGARIAN EMPIRE: POPULATION 50 MILLION, AN ARMY OF 450,000 SOLDIERS

SERBIA

BULGARIA

TURKEY: POPULATION PERHAPS 20 MILLION, AN ARMY OF 210,000 SOLDIERS

ROYAL RELATIONS

Most of Europe's monarchs were related to each other. This should have helped to sort problems out, but it didn't. The monarchs were either mad, stupid or proud - or all three.

Kaiser Wilhelm of Germany (1859-1941) was a grandson of Queen Victoria  and a cousin of the British king, but he loathed the British. He had a withered left arm and a big moustache which was waxed by his special barber every morning. He was mad, proud - and nasty. He liked to hurt people with his extra-strong handshake (with his right hand naturally). He was also stupid and spoiled.

The famous German Chancellor Bismarck said that 'Wilhelm would have liked to have had a birthday every day'. Wilhelm sacked Bismarck in 1890.

Czar Nicholas II of Russia (1868-1918) tried to run his enormous empire single handed because he believed that his power was given to him by God, but he was too stupid to make a good job of it. He liked keeping fit and loved to wear fancy military uniforms.

 Victoria was Queen of Great Britain and Ireland 1837-1901.

Franz Josef I, Emperor of Austria-Hungary (1830-1916) wasn't mad, stupid or proud. He was just incredibly old. He died before the war was over.

George V of Great Britain (1865-1936) wasn't mad or stupid - but he was very proud of his country.

THE KNITTING UNRAVELS

After Austria declared war on Serbia, nothing much happened for a couple of days. At the time both President Poincaré of France and Kaiser Wilhelm were on ships sailing back to their own countries, and the Austrian Emperor Franz Josef was actually on holiday. But then, after they all got home, things happened very fast indeed.

- ✻ *28 July*, Austria declared war on Serbia.
- ✻ *1 August*, Germany declared war on Russia.
- ✻ *3 August*, Germany declared war on France.
- ✻ *4 August*, Germany invaded neutral Belgium en route to France.
- ✻ *4 August*, Britain came to the aid of Belgium and declared war on Germany.

As British Foreign Secretary, Lord Grey, put it:

The lamps are going out all over Europe: we shall not see them lit again in our lifetime.

ORDER YOUR STARTERS

There are three possible answers to each of
the following questions: either correct,
possible or just plain daft. The correct one
should come first and the daft one should
come last - put them in the right order.
(Answers on page 123.)

1 What did the Austrian Empire
do to Bosnia?

a Demolished it
b Swallowed it up
c Declared war on it

2 What was the Black Hand Gang?

a A secret Serbian society
b A gang of Serbian miners
c A secret German society

3 What did Kaiser Wilhelm want
every day?

a A new moustache
b A birthday
c A letter from Queen Victoria

IT'LL BE OVER BY CHRISTMAS

WAR FEVER
A ROOMFUL OF RUMOURS

When Britain declared war on Germany on 4 August 1914, the whole country became madly excited. The air was full of rumours:

A German grocer living in England had been caught selling poisoned food to his customers.

A German barber in England was planning to cut his customers' throats.

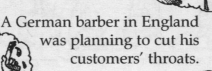

A massive naval battle had been fought in the North Sea.

German spies were everywhere, taking notes and photographs.

A secret Russian troop train had crossed England with drawn blinds, bound for France.

Actually, there was no need for rumours. Reality was bad enough. Germans living in Britain rushed to leave. It wasn't sensible to be a foreigner. 'Aliens', as foreigners are often called, lost their jobs and their homes were attacked. It was very unfair. Many were sent to 'internment camps' - prisons in all but name.

Richard Noschke had lived in Britain for twenty-five years. As a German he was sent to an internment camp in London. This is what he said:

I had made many friends as I had spent the best part of my life over there (in Britain) ... nearly all, with very few exceptions, have turned against me ...

WAR FEVER

As soon as war was declared, thousands upon thousands of British men rushed to join the army, including many from Scotland, Wales and Ireland, which was then part of Britain. The whole country became a giant recruiting station. 30,000 men per day were joining the army by the end of the first month. There was a *two mile* queue to join the Liverpool Scottish regiment.

Sometimes large groups of men from one type of work or from the same town all joined up together in what became known as 'Pals' Battalions'. Pals' battalions had names such as the 'Grimsby Chums'. There weren't enough uniforms to go round so men wore their everyday clothes. Everyone mucked in: business men rubbed shoulders with dustmen, and servants mixed with posh gentlemen. The playgrounds and parks of Britain rang to the sound of men learning to be soldiers.

Men allowed themselves to be swept up in war fever for all kinds of reasons.

They wanted to see if they would be brave enough.

They wanted to travel abroad.

They liked the idea of fresh air and adventure - especially if they had worked in a factory or an office.

War fever wasn't just a British disease. It raged all over Europe. Poets had a field day writing about it all. Over

1.5 million poems were written in Germany and Austria that August - that's 50,000 poems a day! Here's a pretty silly patriotic poem. It was printed on a postcard:

> Would I have my lover back again?
> Yes, when the fight is o'er
> When duty's done and honour's won -
> But never a day before;
> For I could not love him as I do,
> Were he not lover and hero too.

YOUR COUNTRY NEEDS YOU!

Going to war almost seemed like fun. After all, it would be 'over by Christmas'. Everyone said so. Well, not everyone - Lord Kitchener, the British Secretary of State for War, didn't think so. He thought that the war would be long and bloody. In the first months of the War, Kitchener led the British war effort almost single-handedly.

In 1914, Britain was the only large country which didn't have conscription . The British army was puny compared to other armies. So Kitchener prepared for the long struggle by raising brand new 'Kitchener armies' to help Britain's small regular army, which only had 250,000 men compared to Germany's 850,000, France's 700,000 and Russia's million. He did everything he could to encourage men to join up.

Patriotism is love of one's country. A poem which is *patriotic* is about *patriotism*.

Conscription is compulsory military service.

54 million copies of his famous posters were printed - a picture of himself pointing with words such as: 'Britons. Join Your Country's Army! God Save the King'. Thanks to Kitchener, the British army put on muscle fast - a million men had joined up by the end of the year.

BRITONS

YOU

JOIN YOUR COUNTRY'S ARMY!
COD SAVE THE KING

CAN WE JOIN?

Nowadays empires are out of fashion. That wasn't the case back in 1914. Both Britain and France had large empires and the British Empire at that time was the largest empire the world has ever known. British colonists in Australia, New Zealand, Canada and South Africa joined up in their thousands. Likewise, soldiers from the Indian army and from other smaller countries were proud to fight for Britain or France.

As well as soldiers, the countries of Asia and Africa sent large armies of labourers to help the war effort. These men were not as well treated as the regular soldiers. African labourers in France only got half the pay of regular soldiers.

Many British people - English, Irish, Welsh and Scottish - had emigrated to countries in the British Empire, which is why most people in those countries speak English today. Such people were called *colonists* and their countries were called the *colonies*. In 1914 many of them still had close relatives in Britain and thought of themselves as British.

GRUNT, BOO, MOO

Animals were recruited as well. During the course of the war, 100,000 animals, mainly horses and camels, were sent from India to Mesopotamia in the Middle East, where there was fierce fighting. And 50,000 animals, including elephants, were sent from India to the battlefields of Europe and elsewhere.

GOD SAYS

Not everyone was keen to join the army. Some men positively disagreed with the idea.

Posters asked girls to put pressure on their boyfriends to join with clever slogans:

Is your best boy wearing khaki? If not, don't you think he should be?

If he does not think you and your country are worth fighting for - do you think he is worthy of you?

The 'White Feather' movement was launched in Folkestone by an angry admiral. Young women were encouraged to dish out white feathers to young men in civilian clothes as a badge of cowardice.

A civilian is anyone who is not in the armed forces.

Even the Church got in on the act. A Church of England chaplain thought that men who refused to fight ought to be drowned! It was the same all over. The Russian churches prayed:

Most gracious Lord, crush the enemy beneath our feet.

And a German pastor claimed that the slaying of the unworthy was an act of charity.

God must have been in a bit of a muddle about which side he was supposed to be on.

PASTY FACES

In Britain, men who thought it was wrong to fight became known as 'conscientious objectors', 'conchies' for short.

Conchies were savagely treated and many of them were forced to join the army anyway. Six thousand men were sent to British prisons and seventy died there through bad treatment.

However, far from being cowards, conchies were mostly very brave to stand up against public opinion at a time of war fever. In fact, many of them risked their lives driving ambulances in the battle zones anyway. They kept their spirits up through their own newspaper, called the *Dreadnought*. *Dreadnought's* big scoop came later in the war: a letter from the famous poet, Siegfried Sassoon, who had won medals for bravery in France:

I believe the war is being deliberately prolonged by those who have the power to end it ...

Sassoon was sent to a mental hospital which was where a lot of conchies ended up. *Dreadnought* also reported cruelties, such as Field Punishment No.1 for British soldiers. Victims were strapped on to crucifixes on French main roads for up to two hours at a time.

Conchies disagreed with the war but how could the protests of a few thousand stop the catastrophe which was about to happen? All over Europe the new soldiers sang as they marched to the troop trains. In Germany they called their train the 'Paris Express' because they meant to conquer France. They were given garlands of flowers - like cattle before a sacrifice.

WAR FEVER

The date is August 1914. Britain has just declared war on Germany. Each correct answer wins you two degrees on the thermometer - can you reach fever pitch?

(Answers on page 123.)

1 What was the air full of in August 1914?

a German bombers

b Rumours

c The smell of gunpowder

2 What didn't Britain have when the war started?

a A powerful navy

b A border with Russia

c Conscription

3 What were conchies?

a A type of sea shell

b Men who objected to fighting because of their principles

c Men who volunteered to fight for their country

4 Where is this alien going?

a On holiday

b To an internment camp

c To join the British army

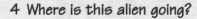

FEVER PITCH

100

99

98

97

96

95

94

33

IT'S A LONG, LONG WAY ...

LET BATTLE COMMENCE

ALL ABOARD!

British soldiers had to cross the English Channel before they could get to the 'front'  in France and Belgium, where the armies faced each other and the fighting would take place. Kaiser Wilhelm is said to have called the British army a 'contemptible little army' because it had so few soldiers in it compared to his own army. From then on, those first British soldiers to enter the war wore the name 'Old Contemptibles' with pride. One popular song of the time went:

Oh, we don't want to lose you
But we think you ought to go ...

It was about saying goodbye to soldiers going to war but the soldiers sang it too.

'*Front*' is short for 'front line' where the fighting took place. See pages 45-46.

Meanwhile, Kitchener's new recruits finished their training, first in Britain and then at Etaples, or 'Eat-Apples' as they called it, a tough training camp south of Boulogne in France. Eat-Apples was a grim place where bullying sergeant majors forced men to march up and down for hour after hour in the 'Bull-Ring', an enormous parade ground.

From Etaples, the journey to the front in France was long and hard, especially for soldiers who were new to soldiering. Simply moving so many men from A to B was a major problem. A division of twelve thousand men with all their gear took a *thousand* railway carriages.

Some French trains were just cattle trucks with straw on the floor. One old soldier described a truck with a notice on it: '40 men - 8 horses'. He spent the whole journey worrying that he was going to have to share his place with a horse!

Things weren't much better for the officers. One carriage had no door so the cold air blew in. The officers had to jump out every so often and run beside the train so as to get warm.

When a division got to the end of the railway line, the soldiers had to get out and march the last bit of the journey to the battle grounds on foot - fifty minutes marching with ten minutes rest every hour. The packs on their backs weighed up to twenty-seven kilos. It was so tough that some men died on the march. Here's what Lance Corporal Mountfort of the Royal Fusiliers had to say about it:

The French roads are horrible. Through every village and for a mile or two on each side they are composed of great rough cobble stones. The nails of our boots step on them as on ice ... Our packs I cannot find words to describe. It is a cruel unnatural weight that no man should be called upon to carry.

The army gave the men tips on how to look after their feet:

Wash well with soap and water.

Dry well.

Rub inside of socks with soft or yellow soap.

Marching was awful and the soldiers tried to laugh away their troubles. One officer had to stop his men making 'excessively rude remarks to people who passed on bicycles'.

LET BATTLE COMMENCE

The Germans had a plan, called the *Schlieffen Plan* after the general who invented it. They planned to attack first - which was a bit like committing suicide in order to avoid dying, considering how many enemies they had. They would invade France through Belgium, beat the French and then attack the massive Russian army in the east.

German soldiers poured into Belgium.

The Germans took Brussels, the capital of Belgium, on 20 August 1914. King Albert of Belgium and his small army holed up in Antwerp near the coast opposite England to wait for the British.

The German occupation of Belgium was brutal. Thousands of Belgian civilians were shot in cold blood. Many Belgian men were herded into cattle trucks and sent to Germany. To cap it all, the Germans sacked the city of Louvain, deliberately burning its wonderful library of 230,000 books - and Belgium was neutral !

When the citizens of Roubaix refused to make sandbags to protect the German trenches, the Germans shot some of them. The citizens said:

We shall not spin winding sheets ✂ for our children.

A *neutral* country does not take part in any wars.
Winding sheets are used to wrap dead bodies.

British newspapers wrote stories about German 'frightfulness'. They said the Germans had built a corpse factory where Belgian bodies were melted down for fat. Most of what the newspapers wrote was bunkum, but British horror was real enough when the Germans executed an English nurse called Edith Cavill who had been helping Belgian soldiers to escape.

Back in Germany, the Germans also read about 'frightfulness' - except it wasn't German frightfulness, it was Belgian. One famous writer described Belgian priests who

... armed, lead bands of Belgian civilians committing every kind of atrocity ... eyes pierced and tongues cut off, of poisoned wells and other horrors.

That was all bunkum as well.

The first clash

On 23 August 1914, the German army came up against the British army for the first time, outside the little Belgian town of Mons. The small British Expeditionary Force fought bravely, but were forced to retreat. The Germans invaded France itself.

The Battle of the Marne was fought a little to the north of Paris starting on 6 September. It involved *two million* men. In that battle and in the next battle, known as the First Battle of Ypres, the French and the small British army stopped the Germans in their tracks.

Angels

Soldiers fighting for their lives sometimes became very superstitious. The story of the *Angels of Mons* was just that - a story - but it was believed as truth by many. British troops retreating from Mons were said to have been protected by the ghosts of medieval English bowmen from the Battle of Crecy, fought between the English and the French in 1346.

An Austrian volunteer in the German army at the First Battle of Ypres was given the Iron Cross and promoted to corporal for his bravery. He was a battalion 'runner', which meant that during the battle he was almost constantly in danger from allied fire. His name was Adolf Hitler - the same Hitler who led Germany during the Second World War.

After the Battle of the Marne, the Germans had a problem. After all, their plan had been to slice through Belgium, beat the French and British in the west, and then turn on the Russians in the east. Well, they hadn't beaten the French and the British, so what should they do next?

The Kaiser sweated over maps of the campaign in his headquarters in Berlin. He sacked his top general.

Then, on 30 August 1914, the Germans beat the Russians at the Battle of Tannenberg in East Germany. 30,000 Russians were killed, partly because they sent radio messages without putting them in code. Throughout the battle, the Germans knew exactly what the Russians were going to do before they did it.

ENTER THE DREADFUL DUO

However, the real victors of Tannenberg weren't the Germans. They were two German generals called Paul von Hindenburg and Erich Ludendorff. Paul von Hindenburg was commander of the German Eighth Army which won the battle of Tannenberg, and Ludendorff was his Chief of Staff. These two men joined up to form a double-act for the rest of the war. They went together like cheese and pickle - except that the pickle was off and the cheese was mouldy. Later, these two generals became the two most powerful men in Germany, more powerful than the Kaiser himself.

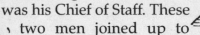

Hindenburg was a retired Prussian 🔫 general. He came from an old noble family. He loved food, drink and cigars. He was very vain and liked to have his portrait painted as often as possible, usually in uniforms with lots of gold braid, decorations and buttons. 'A coat without a button is like a flower without a scent', he told one artist who painted him. What he was best at was never looking ruffled when the going got tough. He always appeared to be in command even when he didn't know what was going on - which happened quite a lot.

Erich Ludendorff was a cold fish - very cold. He had less sense of humour than a haddock. He wore a monocle (single eyeglass) and had a red face and droopy jowls which wobbled when he lost his temper. He was rude and cross most of the time, but he was also clever and very hard-working. Just the sort of man that Hindenburg needed. Their double-act worked like this:

Ludendorff did all the work.
Hindenburg looked important.

The funny thing is that Hindenburg *was* more important than Ludendorff - because he looked more

 Prussia was a former German kingdom. Most of the original Prussian territories are now in Poland or Russia.

important. The Dreadful Duo rose to command all Germany's armies, and by the end of the war they ran Germany itself. It was only at the very end that they fell out - but more on that later.

LIFE IN MUD

TRENCH TROUBLES

MEANWHILE, IN THE MAZE ...

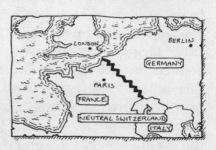

Christmas came and went. So did new year 1915. The line between the enemy armies stretched from the English Channel to the border of Switzerland. The soldiers dug trenches in which to hide from enemy fire, and the front line became a five-hundred-mile scar of trenches and defences dug across the heart of Europe.

The important thing was for the soldiers to keep their heads down and out of the way of bullets. Supplies had to be brought up, meals cooked, rifles cleaned - everything had to be done below ground level. Communicating trenches joined the firing trenches to support trenches further back, and joined them to the reserve lines which were still further back. British trenches followed a zigzag path to deaden the shock waves of exploding shells.

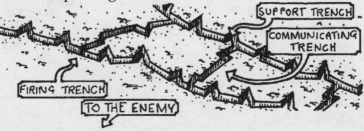

Because the trenches were below ground level, there was nowhere lower down for water to drain into if it rained. As a result, the trenches were often horribly muddy. Wooden 'duck boards' laid along the trench bottoms were supposed to help, but they too were often covered in mud. In the front firing trenches a step was carved into the earth on the side facing the enemy. Soldiers would step up on to this when they wanted to peer over or when it was their turn to fire at the enemy.

FIRESTEP

WOODEN DUCK BOARDS

Life in the trenches in the First World War was incredibly dangerous and uncomfortable. The conditions were truly horrible. Each month British soldiers spent one week in the firing line, one week in the support trenches, one week in the reserve lines and one week behind the lines. Any longer at the firing line and commanders feared that men might go mad or desert. As it turned out, very few of them deserted but quite a lot went mad.

ATTACKS AND SCRAPS

The whole point of being in France was to fight the enemy. The French and British wanted to drive the Germans back into Germany and the Germans wanted to conquer France. Either way, the target was to capture land from the opposition and thus force them to retreat.

In order to win land it was no good just staying in your trench - you had to *attack*. Throughout the war the generals kept organising major attacks when hundreds of thousands of men would be ordered to climb out of their trenches and attack the enemy's trenches - while the enemy naturally tried to stop them. If the attackers managed to hang on to a bit of land which had been controlled by the other side before the attack started, that was called a victory. Often the 'victories' involved pathetically narrow strips of land for which thousands of men paid with their lives.

It was impossible to organise major attacks all the time. They were hideously bloody and exhausting. To keep the men on their toes, and because there was a war going on, the generals organised raiding parties against enemy trenches, gunfire and sniping.
Sectors of the front where there was a lot of that sort of thing were called 'active'.
Sectors where there wasn't were called 'cushy'. Most soldiers from both sides preferred the cushy sectors - understandably enough.

 A *sniper* is an individual soldier with a rifle who aims at individual targets. What he does is called *sniping*.

LIFE - BUT NOT AS WE KNOW IT

If there were no major attacks going on, life in the trenches always settled down to a routine. Half an hour before sunrise might come the order to 'stand to' when each platoon stepped up to the firestep and sentries were posted. Then came breakfast. The day was filled with boring repair work, doing nothing and inspections and there was a second 'stand to' at dusk when the evening rations arrived.

German commanders made sure their trenches were reasonably comfortable, but British commanders didn't believe in making trenches too comfortable in case the soldiers decided to settle down and didn't fight hard enough. This was a pretty nasty attitude to take towards men who, for most of the war anyway, had *volunteered* to fight for their country! Some trenches were so shallow that the men had to walk around stooped over, in order to avoid getting their heads shot off. If it rained, the trenches sloshed with mud. The soldiers shared the mud with trench rats, and with the bones of some of the millions of men who died in battle.

The bones were one of the most horrible things about the trenches. The bodies of soldiers who had died in earlier battles were often churned up again by artillery shells, so that some dead bodies were buried and reburied many times, during the course of the war.

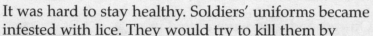

It was hard to stay healthy. Soldiers' uniforms became infested with lice. They would try to kill them by running lighted matches down the seams, but nothing really worked.

Trench fever was a new and dangerous disease. Even worse was trench foot. This appalling illness was caused by spending weeks in cold, wet mud. Feet swelled up to two or three times normal size and went so numb that they could be run through by a bayonet without pain.

OFFICER MATERIAL

Young officers were expected to lead their men into battle. On average, a young officer arriving at the front could expect to live no more than two weeks. In the early days they went into battle with their white gloves on. The Germans could see who they were and so shot them first. These young officers were some of the real heroes. There were mutinies (revolts against authority) in all the other armies, but there were no real mutinies in the British army. The young officers shared the hardships of the common soldiers and many of them truly cared for the men under their command. Letters home from officers were full of requests for chocolate and other luxuries, not for themselves but for their men.

Officers and men were united in hating the generals and staff-officers back at headquarters. One young officer arranged for a trench dam to be 'accidentally' broken so that a general and his staff got covered in slime.

WEAPONS PARADE

A whole package of weapons was available to help the soldiers kill each other.

Artillery was positioned behind the lines. It fired over the heads of the soldiers in the firing line and into the enemy beyond. The biggest guns, such as 'Big Bertha' a type of German gun which bombarded Paris late in the war, could fire up to 122 kilometres (76 miles) or further. The noise from these massive guns was so loud that artillery men might suffer concussion or bleeding ears.

Bayonets were pretty useless in an age of mechanised warfare, but most soldiers carried them.

The main rifle of the British army was the Lee Enfield.

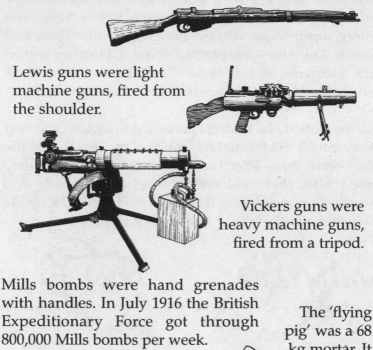

Lewis guns were light machine guns, fired from the shoulder.

Vickers guns were heavy machine guns, fired from a tripod.

Mills bombs were hand grenades with handles. In July 1916 the British Expeditionary Force got through 800,000 Mills bombs per week.

The 'flying pig' was a 68 kg mortar. It could blast through almost any dugout.

Medium-sized mortars were called 'toffee apples' or 'Christmas puddings'.

GAS!

Gas was a new weapon in the Great War. It was first used by the Germans in April 1915 when they gassed a number of French Morrocan soldiers. The murky, greenish-yellow colour of chlorine stained the ground for days afterwards. Chlorine gas was followed by phosgene and then by mustard gas which were even more deadly. Gas caused blindness, suffocation and death. The Allies complained about it, but they copied the Germans all the same. By 1918, a quarter of all shells fired by the armies in France were gas shells.

In the early days, soldiers protected themselves as best they could. Socks soaked in urine and held over the face were quite effective against chlorine. Later they used nose clips and cotton wool mouth pads and finally they were issued with large, heavy gas masks which made them look like mutant elephants.

SINGING MACHINE GUNS

In the Middle Ages, '*nonesmannesland*' meant an area of land where ownership was unclear, then it came to mean a spot outside the walls of the city of London where executions took place. In the Great War, 'no man's land' came to mean the strip of dead ground between the opposing trenches, a ghastly dead place where wounded men often bled to death because it was too dangerous to rescue them. This dead strip of land could be several hundred metres wide, but more often it was less than that. Sometimes the trenches of the opposing armies might only be separated by ten or twenty metres, and sometimes they even ran through the ruins of the same house. When that happened, the men could hear the smallest rustle of their enemies' clothing.

If two armies face each other for over five hundred miles at such close range, there's one thing you can't stop, and it's not killing - it's laughter. The soldiers were human beings after all, and although they had been taught to hate each other before they arrived, it didn't take long for most of them to realise that the enemy were men very much like themselves. On more than one occasion, the war broke down completely. Most famous of these occasions was the Christmas truce of 1914 when the men spilled out of their trenches into no man's land. They gave each other presents, there was a football game and a joint burial service. This is how Rifleman Dick Harvey described it:

The Germans ... they used to walk about on top with our chaps, exchanging cigarettes, tobacco and shaking hands with us. It was a curious sight to see them strolling about in No Man's Land as though war was the last thing they thought about ...

The generals were very cross and it never happened quite like that again.

Quite a few Germans spoke English having worked as waiters in London before the war. They would shout across for news of English football results, or ask the British soldiers to take messages to the Germans' girlfriends in London. One German soldier called across:

It is I Fritz, the bunmaker of London. What is the football news? ... Are you soon going home on leave? Then call at 224 Tottenham Court Road and give my love to Miss Sarah Jones.

There were concerts when the men from each side would sing to each other. Good musicians were popular - no matter which army they belonged to.

A favourite game was for machine gunners to let off bursts of bullets to the rhythm of popular songs. Everyone had to guess what songs they were. A dozen

or more machine guns might join
in the chorus. The British gave
names to Germans who were
good at it:

Duckboard Dick

Parapet Joe

Happy Harry

LIVE AND LET DIE

Douglas Haig (commander of British armies in
France, see page 60) believed in an 'active
front' policy and thought that the men
should keep fighting all the time. So the
front had dangerous sectors where the
fighting never stopped. 'Fire eaters' were
men who wanted to fight. They
weren't popular because the enemy
might fight back! The Scottish
regiments tended to be full of fire
eaters. The Germans called them 'women
from hell' because of their kilts .

Some soldiers actually *enjoyed* fighting. This is what
Lieutenant Colyer had to say about it:

*How different it feels to be doing something! Back there in the
trenches I feel like a rat in a trap ... I don't feel any more
frightened of Fritz (the Germans) than if I were playing hide
and seek in the dark with him ...*

Kilts weren't a good uniform for the trenches. It was found that soldiers
in kilts were more likely to get frostbite and other illnesses. Most Scottish
regiments gave up wearing them.

LIVE AND LET LIVE

On 'cushy' sectors there was almost no fighting at all. Generals didn't approve of cushy sectors but they couldn't do much about them. In cushy sectors, the men on both sides believed in 'live and let live' - they agreed not to kill each other. Above all, they agreed not to fire at each other's toilets and never to fire during breakfast. There were lots of ways of agreeing:

Always fire your guns at the same place at the same time every day. The enemy will soon realise what you're up to and keep out of the way.

Make lots of noise during a raid so the enemy can get out of the way.

Always aim high if an officer orders you to fire your rifle.

Throw over a friendly message tied to a stone, such as this one from some Germans:

We are going to send an 18 kg bomb. We have got to do this but we don't want to - we will whistle first to warn you.

After one burst of artillery fire, a brave German stood up outside his trench and shouted:

We're very sorry about that. We hope no one was hurt. It's not our fault, it's that damn Prussian artillery.

An officer once asked a British soldier why he didn't shoot at an elderly German soldier with a bald head and long white beard whose head was sticking up above the German trenches and made an easy target. The British soldier replied:

Why lord bless you sir, he's never done me any harm!

SOAP AND FOOTBALL

Soldiers were able to relax behind the lines. There the sick and the wounded were treated in field hospitals and the well could enjoy the British soldiers' favourite pastimes of theatre (home-made) and football. There were hundreds of football teams and leagues up and down the front.

Behind the trenches the soldiers found another world, a world where life was almost normal. A world where the French went about their everyday business. In fact British soldiers were amazed at how French farmers would tend their fields almost within shell shot of the Germans. In little French villages the British soldiers could find *estaminets*, small bars where they drank wine - the water was mostly undrinkable. In fact about all that French civilians used water for was washing. Given half a chance the British were no different. Special bath houses were set up for the troops where they could shower in scalding hot water and put on clean clothes without lice - if they were lucky.

CATASTROPHE

AS BAD AS IT GETS

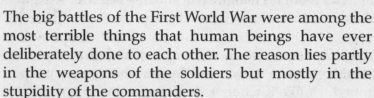

BULLETS V. FLESH

The big battles of the First World War were among the most terrible things that human beings have ever deliberately done to each other. The reason lies partly in the weapons of the soldiers but mostly in the stupidity of the commanders.

One machine gun could kill a line of soldiers in seconds. They had no armour to protect them from the bullets, as armour had once protected soldiers from swords or arrows. So *attack* was difficult because the attackers couldn't defend themselves against the machine guns of the *defenders* (the defenders had their trenches). General Kitchener understood what this meant - that against machine guns, attack was little better than suicide - but he didn't know what to do about it.

Yet there seemed to be no way to win the war other than by attacking the enemy trenches on foot ('going over the top'). Each time the generals gave the order to attack, they knew that thousands of men would die.

It was hopeless. Back home, the politicians complained about the stalemate or the deaths, and sometimes about both. Then on 17 December 1915, they appointed a new man to take over command of the British armies in France. Kitchener at least understood the problem - General Douglas Haig couldn't really see the problem at all.

Like Kitchener, Douglas Haig realised that the war would go on a great deal longer than most people hoped. Unlike Kitchener, he thought it was possible to win it - so long as the British and their French allies had enough guns and ammunition to do the job. In other words, he was ready to command a ghastly slogging match which would cost millions of lives.

THE GRINDING MACHINE

In December 1915, after the slogging match had gone on for over twelve months, the German commanders decided that they would have to 'bleed France white' - the French army was still far larger than the British. It was just a question of numbers: Germany had more men than France, so the French would have to give up first. If necessary, the war would be over when the last German killed the last Frenchman.

This horrible idea was known as 'attrition' and for a

while generals on both sides of the war believed in it. The Germans attacked the fortress of Verdun 200 km (125 m) to the east of Paris, which they knew the French would defend at all costs. The plan was that Verdun would be a killing ground where German forces would slowly destroy the French.

The battle started in February 1916. A *million* German shells  fell on the first day alone. Another million were fired before the German troops attacked. However, to their amazement they found that some French troops had survived the shells and were waiting for them.

And so it went on. For ten dreadful months the Germans flung themselves against the French defences and the French fought back like cornered rats. The French lost *half a million* men - dead, wounded or missing; German losses weren't much better. Verdun became known as the 'mill' or the 'grinding machine'. No one could stay in that hell for long without cracking, so the French commanders sent in new troops and shipped out survivors for a rest - like a giant conveyor belt. By the end of the Battle of Verdun, almost the entire French army had fought in it.

 Shells are large explosive missiles fired from guns.

ORDERS IS ORDERS

First World War armies were too big for their boots - literally. Headquarters, where the generals made their plans and gave their orders, were usually far behind the front line, out of reach of enemy artillery fire. It took ages for an order from headquarters to reach soldiers at the front. No way could a commander decide on an attack and expect it to be carried out the same day. To make matters worse, telephone lines near the front were often cut by shell fire, so to send orders to their troops, generals often had to use runners - in boots - or pigeons.

The size of the armies meant that orders became incredibly complicated. Each group of soldiers, each battery of guns, each group of supply waggons had to be told exactly where to go and what to do. A major attack using tanks, planes, guns and troops needed hundreds, if not thousands, of orders to set in motion. Before the Battle of the Somme, one British headquarters produced a *seventy-six page* plan of attack, backed up by a 365 page supplement!

A HOST OF BEES

Verdun was a French nightmare. The Battle of the Somme was a British nightmare - and a German one. In July 1916, Haig ordered a massive attack across the river Somme in western France so as to draw the Germans away from Verdun and give the French a chance to recover.

The roar of the British guns was so loud that it could be heard back in England. Even the rats in the German trenches panicked.

Well, the rats panicked but not the Germans themselves. They hid in their bunkers, nine metres

Bunkers were underground rooms which the soldiers carved out of the ground. They gave protection from shell fire and rain.

underground, and waited for the bombardment to finish. On 1 June, a beautiful sunny day, the guns fell silent and at the word of command, the British soldiers began the attack. They climbed out of their trenches - going 'over the top' was what they called it - and walked into a blizzard of German machine gun bullets.

One soldier described the sound of the bullets as like the humming of 'hosts of bees'. Photographs show the British soldiers walking forward into the bullets bent forwards almost as if they are walking into a snow storm. *60,000* British soldiers were killed on the first day alone - that's probably around *eighty lives per minute* during the fighting.

The Battle of the Somme raged for over five months - and at the end of it all, the line between the armies was roughly where it had been at the beginning. By the time it was over in November 1916, the Germans had lost 750,000 men, the British 420,000 and the French 195,000.

It was the grim duty of officers to write to the families of the dead. After the Battle of the Somme, people came to dread any knock at the door in case it brought bad news:

> *Dear Sir,*
> *It is my painful duty to acquaint you of the death of your son killed in action on ... there is little comfort that I can add ...*

AND THE WOMEN WORE BLACK

Verdun and the Somme changed how people saw the war. The newspapers could no longer pretend that it was all a wonderful adventure. In Britain, crowds gathered round the offices of their local newspapers and demanded to be told the truth. Lists of the dead began to fill the pages, often with photographs of the young men who had died. Whole streets drew their curtains in mourning. The country looked dingy. Most people wore dark clothes because they were in mourning, and it became unpatriotic to look smart. Smartly-dressed people were jostled in the street.

The Somme also signalled the end of the pals' battalions. The towns where they'd been recruited were devastated by the battle. Some towns lost nearly all their young men in a few short hours of fighting. It was thought better to spread the losses around in future.

DREADFUL DUO (CONTINUED)

Hindenburg and Ludendorff, the victors of Tannenberg, wanted to command all the German armies. After Verdun, Hindenburg became chief of the 'Great General Staff' and Ludendorff became 'First Quartermaster General'. It was even agreed that Hindenburg could give orders in the Kaiser's name without asking him first. The reign of the Duo had begun.

The Kaiser didn't like the Dreadful Duo, but they were popular and he wasn't. While German soldiers were dying by the thousand at Verdun he moved into a different palace, (he had seventy-six of them including castles and hunting lodges) and his life went on as before - like one long holiday. It was all you could expect from a mad man. His favourite hobby was sawing wood. He took up hunting and held champagne dinners for victory. As one German general put it: 'he performed none of the duties of a monarch'.

FRANCE 1917

Ludendorff wisely ordered his troops to dig in and let the enemy attack them, rather than do the attacking themselves. Early in 1917 the German army in France retreated behind the 'Hindenburg line', a new network of trenches.

The retreating Germans laid waste to the land as they left it. Villages and towns were sacked, roads were mined, buildings booby-trapped, wells ruined with horse manure, and most of the people who lived in the area were shipped off to Germany or Belgium.

The French general Nivelle ordered a new attack. The Battle of Chemin des Dames, called after a road to the north of Rheims, was yet another blood bath. The Germans fought back from their new trenches and the French attackers were mown down like grass before a lawn mower. The French won just 500 metres of land and lost 270,000 men in the process.

The horror of seeing large numbers of dead bodies shocked even hardened soldiers. Take this description by a Captain Leetham in 1916:

... the dead were stretched out on one side, one on top of the other, six feet high. I thought at the time I should never get the peculiar, disgusting smell of warm human blood heated by the sun out of my nostrils.

Passchendaele - the victory of mud

British General Haig could have learned from the French disaster at Chemin des Dames. But no - he ordered an all-out British attack.

First, British soldiers dug nineteen tunnels beneath the German lines along Messine ridge, south of Ypres, in Belgium. They packed them with over *half a million kilos* of high explosive.

On 7 June 1917, a massive explosion ripped through the German trenches, killing or wounding twenty thousand men in seconds. It was heard 209 kilometres (130 miles) away in London. Then the British guns opened up and, while the ground was still trembling, 80,000 British soldiers charged out of their trenches. It was a British victory; it was also the start of a journey into hell.

The actual Third Battle of Ypres, otherwise known as Passchendaele, began on 31 July 1917 in the same area. For two weeks before it started, the British guns rained 4.5 million shells on the Germans. This turned out to be a pretty good warning to the Germans that an attack was coming. So when the British attacked, they too were mown down in their thousands.

Haig had been warned to expect heavy rain in that area in August, but he chose to ignore the warning. The guns and the rain churned the battlefield into a huge sea of mud. It was so deep that men and horses drowned in it.

When the attack fizzled out four months later, just outside the village of Passchendaele, the British had gained just over 7 kilometres (4 miles) of ground - and paid for it with the lives of 324,000 men.

IN THE AIR

BIPLANES AND AIRSHIPS

ZEPPELINS

Planes had never been used in war before the First World War. In fact, the first manned flight had only taken place in 1903, so they were a very recent invention. At the start of the war, the French had just 136 and the Germans 180. The British had even less. They proved to be so useful that, by the end, France alone was building more than 136 planes *per day*.

To begin with, the Germans preferred airships. These gas-filled, lighter-than-air monsters weren't as fast as aeroplanes, but they could carry far more bombs and fly much higher. The best were designed by Count von Zeppelin. When they appeared over the British skies people would shout: 'Zeps! Zeps!' as they ran for cover.

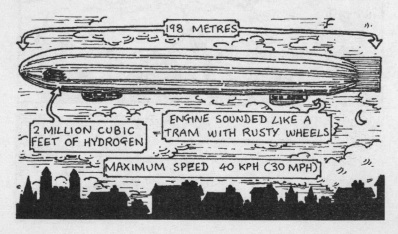

198 METRES

ENGINE SOUNDED LIKE A TRAM WITH RUSTY WHEELS

2 MILLION CUBIC FEET OF HYDROGEN

MAXIMUM SPEED 40 KPH (30 MPH)

At the start of the air war, even the poor mad Kaiser had doubts about dropping bombs on civilians miles behind the scene of battle. But early in 1915, he overcame his doubts and allowed zeppelins to carry out their first bombing mission. They were told to bomb only military targets and to be especially careful not to hit any royal palaces.

The first two raiders were spotted high above East Anglia in January 1915, so high up that they looked like 'two bright stars'. The crash of the bombs from the stillness of the sky was shocking. Four people died. Despite the frightfulness and the danger, there was something marvellous about zeppelins. They were so big and they floated so lazily above the rooftops, as if they had all the time in the world. People came out of their houses to watch.

The first zeppelins could only fly as far as East Anglia, but improved designs soon reached London. Curiosity then gave way to panic, but only for a while. A new explosive bullet was invented and on 2 September 1916, one of these bullets hit its target for the first time. A huge fireball from the burning gas lit the sky above London. It was so bright that you could read a newspaper by its light twenty miles away. The stricken airship turned nose down and the pilot jumped from his gondola to escape the flames. To no avail: his spread-eagled body formed a crater in the soil several centimetres deep. That day spelled the end of airships.

LIGHTS OUT!

Meanwhile the Germans had developed a new deadly weapon - the long distance bomber. The first bomber attack on London came in 1916. Next year, twin-engined Gothas raided deep over England like swarms of 'bright silver insects'.

The bombers caused mayhem and the British had to develop new defences.

Listening posts (which looked like giant ear trumpets) were set up along the coast to give advance warning.

Boy scouts and girl guides worked as messengers, stretcher bearers and signallers during air raids.

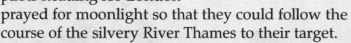

Each night there was a total blackout across Britain. All windows were covered and no street lights were lit. German pilots heading for London prayed for moonlight so that they could follow the course of the silvery River Thames to their target.

WINGS OF FIRE

Where aeroplanes were most useful was over the battlefields of France. They brought back priceless information about enemy positions. Control of the skies had become vitally important for the armies underneath. During the course of the war, 50,000 young men met their deaths in the air. Incredibly brave pilots often shot at each other from less than a hundred metres apart. By 1917, a new pilot arriving in the war zone was not expected to survive more than *seventeen* days. This wasn't helped by the fact that parachutes weren't allowed until the very end of the war, in case airmen were tempted to bail out too soon. The stupidity of World War I commanders was almost boundless.

GENTLEMEN OF THE AIR

Although aircraft were new, the war in the air was in some ways more old fashioned and good-mannered than war on the ground.

Pilots would stop firing at an enemy plane once it was obviously out of action.

When an airman met his death, his enemy would try to honour him by flying over the spot and dropping a wreath.

Flying very high to avoid anti-aircraft fire, pilots would drop messages in metal canisters behind enemy lines asking for news of missing men. Such messages nearly always got a reply.

If an airman had to land in enemy territory, he was normally well treated. In case of capture, most airmen flew with a parcel of such things as pyjamas, toothpaste, cigarettes and money.

PLANES OF FAME

Sopwith camel - British

Fokker triplane - German. Fokkers were the first planes to make sure that machine gun fire was in time with the propellor blades so that the bullets didn't hit the blades. Before that, machine guns had to be fired from the side at an angle.

Nieuport - French

Spad - British

Albatross - German

Sopwith pup - British

THE NARROW ESCAPE OF McLEOD AND HAMMOND.

In 1918, both Alan McLeod and his 'observer', Arthur Hammond were attacked by seven German triplanes.

They shot down two enemy planes, but both airmen were wounded.

Their petrol tank was set alight, setting fire to McLeod's wicker seat.

McLeod throttled back and pushed the joystick forward. He stepped out on to the lower wing to avoid the fire - and kept on flying.

One German aircraft attacked again. The floor below Hammond's cockpit gave way as he struggled to fire back.

Wounded again, Hammond straddled the fuselage and drove off their attacker with his machine gun.

McLeod flew in a curve so that the flames and smoke were blown away from them both.

They landed in a bomb crater. Both survived, although Hammond was wounded in five places.

ACES

The best pilots were called 'aces'. Most famous of all the aces was the German pilot, Baron von Richthofen, otherwise known as the 'Red Baron' because his aircraft was painted red. Von Richthofen's 'circus' of up to thirty aircraft was deadly. He himself shot down eighty enemy aircraft before he was killed by a British airman on 21 April 1918. By then he had become as famous as a sports star. His body was laid out in a British hangar and hundreds of British soldiers and sailors filed past it to pay their respects.

Pilots were mostly very young and, being youngsters, they sometimes got up to mad adventures. New Zealander Keith Park and his observer Puggy Shone bombed the beach at Ostend with oranges where German officers were sitting with their girlfriends.

Later they bombed a German aerodrome with a football painted bright red with streamers tied to it. Their 'bouncing' bomb caused havoc but no injuries.

AIR SLIPS

There's been a bit of a slip-up in each of these pictures. What's wrong with them?
(Answers on page 123.)

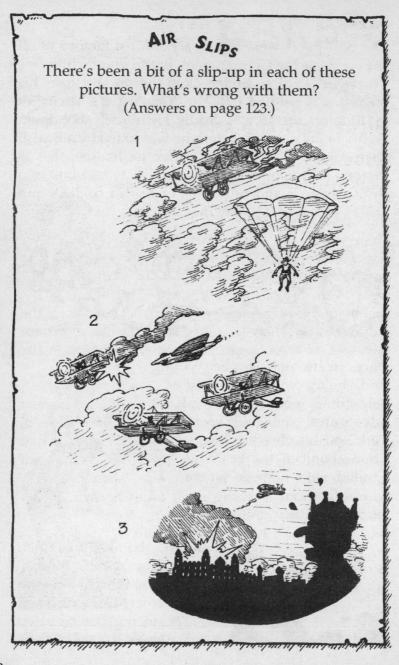

1

2

3

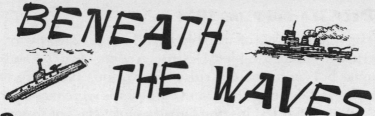

BENEATH THE WAVES

BILGE RATS AND KIPPERS

BILGE RATS

Airmen were aces, soldiers were 'leather-necks' (at least as far as sailors were concerned) and sailors were 'bilge-rats '. There were a lot of bilge rats in the British Royal Navy in 1914. It was then the largest navy in the world. And there were even more bilge rats in the British Merchant Navy, which was also the largest in the world - more than twice as large as the merchant navies of all the other countries which fought in the Great War put together.

Even before the war, the Germans hadn't liked the fact that the British were so strong at sea. As we've seen, the German leadership believed that Germany too had a right to an empire, to a 'place in the Sun' as they put it. They could never hope to win such an empire without a strong navy of their own. Under the leadership of stern, fork-bearded Admiral Tirpitz, they set out to build one. Britain had no intention of letting them catch up, and the arms race which followed had helped to heat the war fever of 1914.

 Bilge water is filthy water that collects in the bilge, the bottom of a ship.

DEEP SEA DUMPLING 1914

The main classes of warship in 1914 were destroyers, cruisers and battleships. Destroyers were very fast and agile but quite small. Cruisers of various types were large, fast fighting ships, and battleships were massive. And of all battleships, the Dreadnought class of super-battleship was most feared. Dreadnoughts were named after *HMS Dreadnought*, launched in 1906. She had twelve massive guns which could fire over 16 kilometres (10 miles) and she displaced 22,000 tons of water. Nothing could stand up to a Dreadnought.

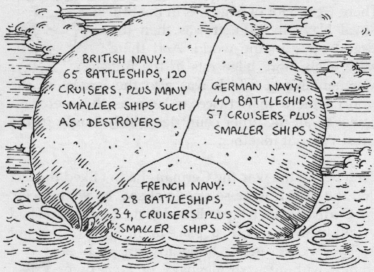

BRITISH NAVY: 65 BATTLESHIPS, 120 CRUISERS, PLUS MANY SMALLER SHIPS SUCH AS DESTROYERS

GERMAN NAVY: 40 BATTLESHIPS 57 CRUISERS, PLUS SMALLER SHIPS

FRENCH NAVY: 28 BATTLESHIPS, 34 CRUISERS PLUS SMALLER SHIPS

The German commanders were well aware that the British navy was more powerful than their own, so the German navy spent almost the entire war holed up in its base at Wilhelmshaven. As a result, there was only one major battle between the main British and German fleets, and that didn't happen until the end of May 1916. There's never been a sea battle of a similar size since. It involved 250 warships.

THE BATTLE OF JUTLAND

On 31 May 1916, British scouting ships off Jutland Bank in the North Sea made contact with German ships. They had no idea that the German fleet was in the area.

The battle started with a fight between cruisers which the Germans got the better of. After that the main fleets clashed.

The main battle lasted only a few minutes but it was spectacular. The guns of the massed battleships and cruisers sent waterspouts gushing up to sixty metres into the air. Direct hits produced vast columns of smoke and debris. The German Admiral soon realised that he was out-gunned. The Germans turned away under a smoke screen and scuttled back to base as fast as they could. From that time on, the German fleet never challenged the British fleet again, not in the First World War anyway. The British had won the argument even if they hadn't triumphed in the battle itself.

The British First Sea Lord in 1915 was Admiral John Fisher. Fisher hated sport, perhaps due to the fact that when young he had shot a butler in mistake for a rabbit.

KILLER KIPPERS

The mighty Dreadnoughts were a threat which were never fully used. Not so 'kippers', or 'tinfish', as submarines were known in the Royal Navy. And especially not German kippers.

German submarines were better designed than British submarines. Even at the start of the war, the best German vessels could diesel at full speed for up to 6,500 kilometres (4000 miles), submerge in less than two minutes to a depth of 30-60 metres, and travel for up to 130 kilometres (80 miles) underwater.

In other words, they could pop up almost anywhere, let off their torpedoes and scarper before the British had time to react.

On 22 September 1914, a German submarine, U-9 , was cruising off the coast of Holland when her captain spied three British cruisers, *HMS Aboukir*, *Cressy* and

---

U-boats were German submarines. The 'U' is short for *Unterseeboot*, meaning 'under-sea ship'.

Hogue. They were very powerful ships and one measly submarine should have been no match for them.

U-9 sank the lot in one hour before breakfast. 1,459 men died, more men than all the British sailors who had died during the entire Battle of Trafalgar over a hundred years before.

Less than a month later, a single German U-boat was spotted in a Scottish loch. After their experience off Holland, the British took no chances. Due to this one U-boat, Scapa Flow, the deep-water base of the British fleet, was declared unsafe and the entire fleet was moved to Northern Ireland until Scapa Flow could be made secure. From then on, apart from the Battle of

Jutland, the mighty British navy spent almost all of the War holed up in Scapa Flow, like some monstrous guard dog that couldn't be allowed out of its kennel.

Most submarines used diesel on the surface, although to start with the French preferred steam. But both diesel and steam engines are useless under water because they need air to burn fuel. During the First and Second World Wars, submarines ran on electric motors powered by huge batteries when submerged.

Biggest of all submarines were the British K-boats. K-boats were massive - and pretty useless. Only seventeen K-boats were built - they had sixteen bad accidents and eight disasters. K-boats were far too long and narrow. The Germans had a joke about them:

MY END IS DIVING - WHAT THE HELL IS YOUR END DOING?

LIFE IN A KIPPER

Early submarines were hideously uncomfortable.

Their long, thin hulls rolled badly. Water from the conning tower (the bit that sticks up in the middle of a submarine) mixed with food and vomit from sick submariners and sloshed from side to side.

The underwater toilets stank so horribly that some crew members used to take medicines to stop themselves using them.

Moisture condensed on the steel walls. It would drop onto the faces of sleeping men. It was common practice to sleep with a rubber sheet over the face.

Lack of bunks on British submarines meant that taking turns with bunks was often unavoidable.

Men could get 'drunk' on gasoline fumes from the engines. Mice were kept on board. Their squeaking let the sailors know if any gasoline escaped.

Pressure could build up under water. It was sensible to hold on to the captain's legs when he opened the hatch, to stop him shooting out like a cork from a bottle.

A SINK IN THE DRINK

By 1917 the U-boats were sinking an average of *630,000 tons* of allied shipping per month. On the other hand, the British navy was strong enough to blockade Germany so that almost no goods or food got through by sea. Both countries were being strangled. The question was: who would strangle who first? For quite a while it looked as though Britain might be the loser. The British fought back as best they could:

In clear water a submarine could be seen at quite a depth. British submarines towed 'blimps' or observation balloons, which floated high up. The observer in the small cage could spot U-boats from a distance.

At the beginning of the war, some British torpedo boats carried lengths of copper wire with a noose on the end. The idea was to lasso the enemy's periscope.

Q-boats were designed to look like harmless merchant or fishing vessels. However, if a U-boat attacked one of them the Q-boat quickly showed her teeth.

Gunfire and ramming were thought to be the best ways to sink a U-boat.

A *periscope* is a device which allows you to see round corners (or above the surface if you're under water), using mirrors to reflect light. They were also used to see over the top of trenches without exposing the head of the looker to enemy fire.

CONVOY AHOY!

At last, on 30 April 1917, Britain came up with an answer to submarines - convoys. A convoy consisted of a large number of merchant ships protected by warships. They all sailed together. Lloyd George, the British Prime Minister had been suggesting this for years, as had others such as Winston Churchill, but the admirals had claimed that convoys would be sitting targets for the U-boats. It really was extraordinary how foolish First World War commanders could be.

Almost at once Allied losses at sea started to fall. Convoys had two big advantages:

1. Allied merchant ships were no longer scattered all over the oceans. It was no longer possible for a U-boat to cruise about and expect to bump into its prey by chance. Now the U-boats often failed to bump into anything at all.
2. When a U-boat attacked a convoy, it often only got in one shot, then it had to dive fast or the naval destroyers would sink it.

All in all, convoys were a big success. Between May and November 1918, 1,142 ships carrying 2,079,880

American soldiers plus food and other supplies crossed the Atlantic in convoy, and only one was lost.

THE LOSING OF THE LUSITANIA

On 7 May 1915, the British liner, *Lusitania*, was steaming home to Liverpool from New York. She had two thousand passengers on board and a cargo of ammunition for the British war effort, although that was a secret at the time. The *Lusitania* had just rounded the southern tip of Ireland when she was spotted by the submarine U-20, captained by blond, handsome Walter Schweiger.

Schweiger was no monster but he had his orders. At that time, German submarines were under orders to attack all shipping in the seas around the British Isles and they didn't have to give any warning. Schweiger's first torpedo set off a massive explosion on board the great liner, which keeled over and sank within eighteen minutes. 1,198 people died that day, including 94 children and 128 Americans.

It was the Americans who really mattered. At that time America was neutral, but with the loss of the Lusitania American public opinion started to shift in favour of the Allies. To make matters worse, the German government struck a special medal to gloat over the sinking. The medal was copied in large numbers in America and Britain as proof of yet more German 'frightfulness'.

Blindly, the Germans torpedoed another passenger liner, the *Arabic*, that August, killing three more Americans. There were howls of outrage. For a while the Germans were forced to be more careful, and at least not to attack without warning.

However, by 1917 the Germans were desperately short of food due to the British blockade. Their only chance still seemed to be to starve Britain into asking for peace. On 1 February they declared unrestricted submarine warfare. This was a dangerous move because it was bound to anger the Americans even more.

On 3 February America cut all relations with Germany, and by April, Germany and America were at war.

HOME AT LAST

BACK IN BRITAIN

THE GREEN DREAM

Soldiers in the trenches in France longed for home leave , to be back in 'Blighty' as they called Britain. Unfortunately, the reality of home leave never quite lived up to the dream. After the hell of the trenches, the lush, green English countryside could seem overwhelmingly beautiful at first, but soldiers found it difficult to fit back into ordinary life. The people back home sounded so *warlike*. Hating was easy from far away. It was much harder to hate the enemy if you had sung to him at night and you knew that he suffered as you did. As one soldier put it: 'the further you get from the battle line, the more offensive are the people you meet'.

HOW MANY GERMANS HAVE YOU KILLED?

 In the armed forces 'leave' means permission to be absent from duty.

And did those civilians hate! The Germans even had a 'song of hate'. It went like this:

We will never forgo our hate
We have all but a single hate
We love one, we hate one.
We have one foe and one alone - England!

Meanwhile the bishop of London preached a sermon of hate:

We are banded in a
great crusade - we
cannot deny it - to kill
Germans ... to kill the
good as well as the bad,
to kill the young men
as well as the old ...

DO YOUR BIT

There was no escape from war. Even if you were home on leave, it was all around you. Everyone 'did their bit' for the war effort.

In Germany, school children were told to collect nettles to make into nettle fibre for weaving cloth.

In Britain, schools ran jumble sales and concerts. People collected silver paper and rags to melt down for metal and to make cloth.

There were 'tank banks' to help raise money for arms. A 'Feed the Guns' campaign in London raised £1 million. It was opened by six girls who had lost their boyfriends. They stood by a tank which had the mud of France still on it.

Railway lines were pulled up to be melted down for guns and ammunition.

FOOD – IF YOU CAN GET IT!

Both Germany and Britain ran short of food. It was worst for Germany, where three quarters of a million people died of starvation during the war, especially during the terrible 'turnip winter' of 1917. They imposed a tax on cats in Dresden since cats eat food. Life was hard in Britain too. Every scrap of land that could be dug was turned into allotments. School playing fields, parks and tennis courts, all felt the spade. The king and queen even dug up the gardens of Buckingham Palace.

AND DRINK

Drink was seen as an enemy of the war effort. Once again the Royal Family set an example by giving up alchohol until the war was over. The Great War saw the start of limited drinking hours for pubs, which are still with us today.

Officially it was forbidden to eat crumpets, give bread to dogs, throw rice at weddings or stiffen your collar with starch (among other things), but actually, the rich could, and did, buy most things they wanted on the 'black market 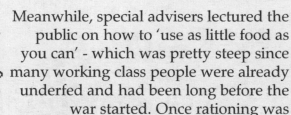 '.

Meanwhile, special advisers lectured the public on how to 'use as little food as you can' - which was pretty steep since many working class people were already underfed and had been long before the war started. Once rationing was introduced later in 1917, if anything, working people ate better than they'd done before because food was more fairly shared out.

 The 'black market' was for food and other items which were sold illegally.

The rations definitely helped. Before long there were rations for almost everything. Lloyd George, the 'New Conductor', had become Prime Minister in 1916. He ran Britain like a war machine. There were twelve different ration cards per person. It was even worse in Europe under the Central Powers. They had a joke about it:

... take a meat card, turn it in an egg card and fry it until nice and brown in a butter card. Cook the potato card and the vegetable card and add the flour card. After the meal one washes oneself with the soap card ...

A DOMESTIC SCENE

This soldier is glad to be back home in the bosom of his family. But someone is doing something they shouldn't. What is it?
(Answer on page 123.)

WHAT WOMEN DID

WE'RE RIGHT BEHIND YOU!

WORKERS, NOT SHIRKERS

Some people claim that men are more warlike than women, and perhaps they're right. But most women supported the Great War to the hilt. Many regretted that they didn't have the chance to fight and die like their men.

Before the war, most women didn't work outside the home. Just looking after the house was hard enough. There were few useful gadgets such as hoovers and washing machines to help out - and men weren't expected to help. Also, families tended to be large. Nine or ten children in a family wasn't uncommon. More children meant more work for their mothers.

Those women that did work outside the home tended to work in 'women's trades', for instance in the clothes industry or as house maids. The First World War changed all that. So many men were away fighting that large numbers of women were needed to do 'men's' jobs. By the end of the war five million women had full time jobs.

So many male farm workers went to war that farm land stood idle. Women's Land Army workers did all the jobs previously done by men. They wore men's clothes because they were more convenient.

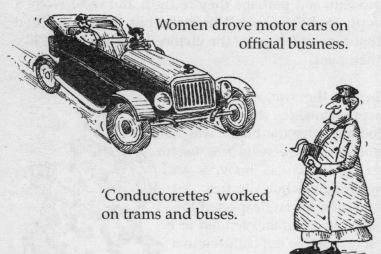

Women drove motor cars on official business.

'Conductorettes' worked on trams and buses.

CANARIES

By the end of the war there were three times as many women as men working in the munitions factories of Britain. 'Munitionettes' worked twelve hour shifts building the guns and packing the explosive shells which flowed in a never-ending stream to the killing fields of France. The girls who worked with TNT, a high explosive, were known as 'canaries' because their faces turned a horrible yellow colour. They worked the 'monkey machines'. Four girls raised a heavy weight which was then dropped on to a mixture of TNT and amatol, packing it into the shell case. There were a lot of accidents.

MONEY, MONEY, MONEY

War meant money - for the workers back home at any rate. A British infantry man in France could be killed for just a shilling a day (5p, but worth more in those days); the girls in the factories could earn *forty shillings* a week. It wasn't fair, but it brought prosperity to many working class homes, especially since many of the older children worked as well. For the first time, many working class girls had money for luxuries. Munitionettes were always being scolded for their love of pretty clothes - and drink. Women's ready-made dress shops boomed while men's tailors went out of business by the bucketful - the men tended to die before they could pay their bills.

ARFA THIMBLE
GENTS TAILOR

War wasn't all bad. Life was short and people were desperate to enjoy it. Dancing was a major craze and the young women took full advantage. All kinds of dance clubs opened in London during the war, it was the same in Berlin and Paris. It was all the more intense as an experience because they never knew what might happen to their partners. A man might dance one day and die the next.

This was a time of growing freedom for women. Skirts were shorter due to the shortage of cloth, hair was shorter due to the danger of long hair getting stuck in machines, and wearing make-up and smoking in public became acceptable.

WAR FOR VOTES

Middle class women leapt at the chance which war gave them to escape the boredom of life stuck at home. In 1914 when the war started, voluntary women's committees in support of the war effort sprang up like dandelions in a cabbage patch. Khaki became a fashionable colour to wear (if you weren't in black for mourning).

As a reward for their support, women won the right to vote. Before the war, the suffragettes (the women who fought for the right to vote) were imprisoned, roughly handled by the police and force-fed when they went on hunger strike. In 1914 when the war started, women still couldn't vote. Despite this, most British suffragettes decided to throw their weight behind the war effort. As their leader Mrs Pankhurst put it: 'What would be the good of a vote without a country to vote in?'

Their gamble paid off. In 1918 when the war was over, women over thirty were given the right to vote. In 1928, this was extended to all women over twenty-one (the same as men).

INTO UNIFORM

More than 100,000 women joined the women's auxiliary services during the Great War. The first time ever that British women served in the armed forces:

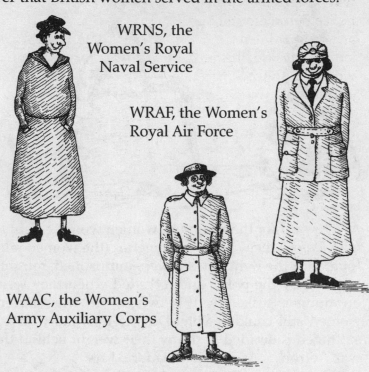

WRNS, the Women's Royal Naval Service

WRAF, the Women's Royal Air Force

WAAC, the Women's Army Auxiliary Corps

The WAAC was the biggest service. *Les tommettes*, as the French called them suffered under petty rules, such as the one that said only officers could wear belts in their raincoats. Married women weren't allowed to serve in the same area as their husbands and barbed wire fences round WAAC camps kept men out and the women in.

The Great War also saw the first women police officers in Britain. Germany had them by 1905, but up until the war started, British policemen were still busy arresting women suffragettes so the idea of women police officers didn't make much sense. The very first English town to make use of women police was Grantham in Lincolnshire.

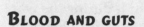

BLOOD AND GUTS

Toughest of all the volunteer services were the VADs, the Voluntary Aid Detachments. The VADs provided 15,000 nursing attendants and 23,000 nurses during the course of the war.

These young girls, often from sheltered middle and upper classes homes, helped men with the most ghastly wounds. They worked in hospitals near the front and lived mainly in tents. Winter was especially difficult. The tents froze rigid in the bitter cold - as did the women's clothes. They had to sleep in their clothes because it was impossible to put them on in the morning if they were frozen stiff.

Medicine came on in leaps and bounds during the war, but routine nursing was still a ghastly trade. Dressings on the worst wounds might have to be changed six times a day. At night the girls might go to bed stinking of pus. If that wasn't enough for them, they had to pick the lice from the uniforms of common soldiers.

AND GUTSY HEROES

The life of a VAD wasn't enough for everyone. Some women craved greater excitement.

Flora Sandes volunteered as a nurse, went to Serbia, served with a Serbian regiment, was wounded by hand grenades and ended up as a sergeant major in the Serbian army.

Mairi Chishholm and Mrs Knocker ran an unofficial first aid post immediately behind the front line. 'The two', as they became known, worked in terrifying conditions. They were frequently shelled and their drinking water, drained from the corpse-strewn ground, was green even after boiling. They treated all who came to them and were awarded the Star of the Order of Leopold II by the Belgian king.

FASHION VICTIM

Two mannequins from before and during the war have got muddled up. Which pieces should go with which? (Answer on page 123.)

LONG HAIR
SHORT HAIR
SMOKING
MAKE-UP
NO MAKE-UP
SHORT SKIRT
LONG SKIRT

BREAK-THROUGH!

THE END IS NIGH

TANKED UP

The way war was fought changed for ever in November 1917. Until then it was impossible for either side to attack without risking huge loss of life from machine gun fire. Tanks were armoured vehicles which protected men as they advanced, and November 1917 was when they were first used successfully. Their steel armour kept out everything except direct hits from artillery. Suddenly attack was no longer an especially unpleasant form of suicide.

But it was no thanks to the army that British soldiers were protected in this way. Given the danger of machine guns, you might think that army commanders would have fallen over themselves to find ways to protect their men during an attack. Well, forget it. Even Kitchener, and he was wiser than most, thought tanks were just mechanical toys. The development of the first tanks was left to the British *Admiralty*, which controls the *navy*, not the army. Winston Churchill, who was First Lord of the Admiralty in the early stages of the war, was almost the only top leader to see how useful tanks would be. The Germans never developed any good tanks until the next World War.

Early designs included a 'land battleship'. It was 30 metres long, 24 metres across and 14 metres high with massive naval guns, and it weighed 300 tons. It was carried on twelve-metre wheels. This huge beast wasn't practical and was never built.

Meanwhile, 'Little Willie' was born . Little Willie was the first proper tank. It had tracks which allowed it to travel across the roughest ground, although it never actually went into service.

Finding a name for the new weapon turned out to be quite a problem. They tried out 'land ship' and 'land cruiser', but felt that such names would give too much away to enemy spies. Without its tracks and guns the new weapon looked a bit like a 'cistern ' or a 'container'. Finally they settled on 'tank' because it meant much the same thing but was a shorter word.

The early tanks came in two sexes: male and female. Males had guns and females had machine guns. They worked together, the female giving supporting fire to the male.

Actually a similar and slightly better design had been suggested by a Mr Mole, an Australian, back in 1912, but no one had taken any notice.

A cistern is a place for storing water - like behind the toilet or in the loft.

Inside a tank

Early tanks were hell to drive. The inside was lit by a dim electric light, the temperature might rise as high as 120° and the guns were so noisy that they could split a man's eardrums. When machine gun bullets hit the outside, they set off an inferno of flying sparks inside. To protect themselves, the crew wore armour-plated masks, with slits for eye holes and chain-mail to cover their chins. They looked like something out of the middle ages.

Cambrai

Tanks were first tried out at the Battle of the Somme in 1916 but were a disappointment. They got bogged down in the mud and there weren't enough of them. This was Haig's fault. No credit to him that this failure turned out to be a blessing in disguise - the Germans decided that tanks were nothing to worry about.

In late 1917, General Haig had suffered yet another bloody set-back at the Third Battle of Ypres (see page 69). He needed a quick victory to 'restore his reputation'. So he decided to give the tank corps another chance.

The town of Cambrai lay just behind German lines in an area of France which hadn't been fought over much, and so hadn't been churned into a sea of mud. It was excellent, firm rolling countryside - ideal for tanks.

The tanks were brought to Cambrai in strict secrecy. They were hidden beneath trees and in bombed-out buildings behind British lines.

The first thing the Germans heard on the morning of 20 November 1917, was the British guns followed by the roar of primitive engines. Then they saw 474 huge, dinosaur-like monsters roll out of the early morning mist towards them. The Germans fired their machine guns but the bullets just bounced off the monsters.

Where the word 'cambric' for a type of fabric comes from, due to the local industry of making fine fabrics.

The machines carried huge bundles of sticks which they dropped into the German trenches, then rolled over them.

In three days the tanks won 8 kilometres (5 miles) of land. Cambrai marked the end of the stalemate in France and the end of the reign of the evil machine gun.

BREAKTHROUGH!

As it turned out, Hindenburg and Ludendorff didn't mind too much about the bad news from Cambrai. They had good news from the east. On 6 November 1917, Bolshevik soldiers and sailors captured St Petersburg, the Russian capital. A new, Bolshevik government took power on the promise of 'no more war', and 6.5 million Russian troops on the eastern front stopped fighting. Germany was now free to move all her troops to the west to fight Britain and France. Hindenburg moved his headquarters nearer to the front line. He took plenty of books to read because, as he wrote to his wife: 'the days will be somewhat long'.

The Bolsheviks were the main revolutionary Russian communist party.

Ludendorff did all the work as usual. He planned to use his troops in small groups of 'storm troopers' backed up by rolling artillery fire.

ROLLING ARTILLERY FIRE

Rolling artillery fire was used to back-up soldiers advancing towards the enemy on foot. As the soldiers moved forwards, shells from their own artillery were fired over their heads from behind them and were aimed to explode continuously about a hundred metres ahead of the soldiers as they advanced.

Hindenburg and Ludendorff wanted this attack to be the big one, the finishing blow against Britain and France. Before the German attack started they ordered the biggest artillery barrage the world has ever seen before or since. Then the Germans blasted their way forwards. By the end of May they'd fought to within 64 kilometres (40 miles) of Paris. It was the biggest breakthrough of the war so far.

However, Ludendorff's big attack ran out of steam. The German army moved too far, too fast and they started to run out of supplies of food and ammunition. The Allies fought them every step of the way and were helped by the Americans who had recently joined the war on their side.

THE YANKS ARE COMING!

When America had declared war on Germany in April 1917, most of the young soldiers didn't know what they were in for. They were given advice such as:

A complete bathing suit comes in handy.

Bring sneakers or slippers - they will add greatly to your comfort after a hard day's march.

Once they got to France they soon learned better.

A BLACK DAY

The German soldiers started to get seriously fed up. Would they ever be able to stop fighting? By July, the great German attack had fizzled out altogether, and on 18 July 1918 the Allied counter-attack began.

Due to the British blockade, the German troops were now down to a diet of dried turnips, horse meat and sawdust spread with a turnip paste known as 'Hindenburg fat'. Many of them lost all interest in fighting. Reports of German surrenders flooded back to German headquarters.

Then came 8 August 1918 - the 'Black Day' of the German army according to Ludendorff. 450 British tanks, backed up by British, Australian and Canadian soldiers captured 16,000 prisoners in a few hours near the old battlefield of the Somme. The Germans had crumbled like soggy biscuit.

LUDENDORFF LOSES IT

The strain of defeat was too much for Ludendorff. He took to drinking too much, crying suddenly and losing his temper for no reason. A doctor ordered rest, massage, no more talking in a high shrill voice of command, and the singing of German folk songs on waking. Amazingly, it worked - for a while.

But the bad news kept flooding in.

30 September 1918, Bulgaria caved in.

24 October - 2 November 1918, the Battle of Vittorio Veneto. Austria lost to the Italians. A quarter of a million Austrian deserters roamed the countryside, looting and pillaging.

27 October 1918, Austria caved in.

Hindenburg and Ludendorff couldn't cope any more. They hid their heads in the sand like camels and tried to pretend that it wasn't happening. They dreamed of a peace treaty which would favour Germany. In their dream treaty, Denmark and Holland would send back all the German deserters who had taken shelter in their countries, and Germany would hang on to the large chunks of eastern Europe which it had conquered during the war.

The dream treaty was pie in the sky. Back in January, President Woodrow Wilson of the USA had come up with fourteen 'points' as the basis for peace. One of

Deserters are soldiers or sailors who have run away from the armed forces. In time of war, deserters are often shot.

these points was that the Germans musn't hang on to any conquered land. Now the Allied peace terms became even tougher. They demanded that the Kaiser must give up his throne, and, worst of all, the Dreadful Duo themselves must go (in polite language of course).

It was awful - for the Dreadful Duo. On 27 October, the day Austria caved in, Ludendorff resigned after a row with the Kaiser. He then had a row with Hindenburg on the steps of the palace. The Duo was a duo no more.

Cinema audiences in Berlin cheered at the news that Ludendorff had resigned.

THE END

Germany itself was crumbling away. Riots broke out all over the place. If the leaders didn't make peace fast, they would have no country left to make peace with - and they couldn't make peace because the Allies refused peace as long as the Kaiser stayed on the throne.

At last, on 9 November, Kaiser Wilhelm gave up his throne. He boarded a special silver train and left for Holland, never to return. Germany and the world heaved a sigh of relief. Two days later, representatives of the German government met Marshal Foch, overall commander of the Allied armies in the west, in a train in the forest of Compiegne in northern France, to sign the armistice .

The war was over.

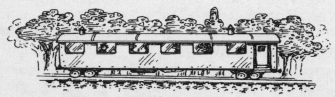

DEATH RIDE

Shortly before the armistice was signed, the admirals of the German navy decided on a 'death ride' - on 28 October, the German navy would sail forth to glorious defeat. But the German sailors weren't having any of it. They were sick and tired of their officers, who had feasted and held drinking bouts right through the war while their crews ate rubbish.

The sailors refused to weigh anchor. Those on ships already at sea put out the boilers. On a steam ship that means the ship can't move.

There was no death ride.

Armistice means an agreement to end the fighting.

114

WHAT WAS † THE POINT?

LOOKING BACK

WHAT A DIN!

The Great War ended at 11.00 am on 11 November 1918 - the eleventh hour of the eleventh day of the eleventh month.

When news of the armistice reached Britain, the whole country exploded with joy. Huge crowds gathered in the streets of London and other big cities. Boy scouts careered through the crowds on their bikes blowing the 'all clear' on their bugles, bells rang, the police blew their whistles. The party went on for three whole days.

Some of the returning soldiers found it hard to join in. Hiram Sturdy was in Glasgow. This is how he put it:

...singing, dancing, yelling people ... the pent-up feelings of four years of waiting, sorrow, loneliness, misery, wickedness, crimes and cruelty of unbelievable magnitude being sung, drunk and danced out.

Flu

As a reminder of the feebleness of people, even at their nastiest, compared to the power of nature, a flu epidemic swept round the world in the winter of 1918/19. Around *twenty-seven million* people are said to have died - *three times the number who died because of the war* - in just a few short months.

No way to treat an enemy

On 28 June 1914, the war had started with the shooting of Archduke Franz Ferdinand in Sarejevo (see page 17). On 28 June 1919, exactly five years and about nine million dead soldiers later, the Treaty of Versailles was signed by defeated Germany.

Germany's nose was in the dirt and the Allies meant to keep it there. At the Treaty of Versailles, Germany and

A *treaty* is a signed agreement between two or more countries.

the other Central Powers agreed to repay every cent of damage caused by the war. This was known as 'reparations' and the final figure was fixed at the huge sum of £6.6 billion plus interest (add at least two noughts for today's value), payable over thirty years.

WHAT HAPPENED NEXT

Reparations were so enormous that Germany couldn't afford to pay them. In 1923 France took control of a chunk of Germany for a while instead.

In 1925 Hindenburg, who should have been retired, was elected president of Germany - and again in 1932. The next year, he chose as his chancellor (like our Prime Minister) another old soldier of the Great War. That soldier's name was Adolf Hitler, now leader of the National Socialist Party of Germany - 'Nazis' for short. Hitler, like many Germans, was still bitter about losing the First World War and about the cost of reparations. Six years later, in 1939, he led the Germans into the Second World War.

It's hard to find anything good to say about the First World War. It did however change the world forever.

In Britain, in the 'Khaki' election which followed victory, Lloyd George (the British Prime Minister) promised a 'land fit for heroes'. It was never a land fit for heroes but there were some changes:

1918, EDUCATION ACT - COMPULSORY EDUCATION TO THE AGE OF 14

1918, VOTES FOR WOMEN OVER 30

1919, MINISTRY OF HEALTH ACT - BETTER HEALTH CARE

1920, UNEMPLOYMENT INSURANCE - THE START OF UNEMPLOYMENT PAY

1921, THE BRITISH LEGION FOUNDED TO HELP OLD SOLDIERS

1928, VOTES FOR WOMEN OVER 21

NINE MILLION DEAD

RED IS FOR REMEMBRANCE

We still live with the First World War. In every town and every village across Europe there's a war memorial with a long, sad list of the dead and in France and Belgium the cemeteries of the war dead go on for miles.

In Britain every year when autumn comes around, we wear red paper poppies in memory of the killing fields of France. And on the eleventh hour of the eleventh day of the eleventh month, when the war ended, we all stand silently for two minutes to show our respect for the dead, and our determination that such a terrible thing must never happen again.

Let's hope it never does.

MEANWHILE, ELSEWHERE ...

This book has concentrated on the war in western Europe between Germany and France and Britain. But the War affected many other countries throughout the rest of the world.

AFRICA was a sideshow in the Great War. Quite small troops of soldiers, mainly African but with European officers, fought it out for control of Germany's few African colonies. Germany lost these colonies at the end of the war as a result of its defeat.

IRELAND was part of Britain in 1914. However, many Irish people wanted their own, independent Irish parliament. In 1916, some took matters into their own hands. The 'Easter Rising' was doomed to fail, but for a while the rebels took control of several buildings in central Dublin, including the central post office. When it was all over, the authorities ruthlessly executed the ringleaders.

The executions shocked the Irish and from then on they tended to become more anti-British. This left the Irishmen who had joined the British army high and dry. Many of them fought and died bravely, but they are sadly forgotten in their own country today.

ITALY was unsure whether or not to join the war in 1914. It joined the Allies in April 1915 and from then on spent the war fighting bravely against Austrian troops along the mountainous border between Italy and the Austro-Hungarian Empire.

RUSSIA lost around 1.8 million men during the Great War - about 12% of all who served in the army, although the war in the east was never quite as stuck in the mud as the war in France. During 1916, under General Brusilov, one of their few good commanders, the Russians fought back against Germany and especially against Austria, but they never really recovered from the defeat at Tannenberg at the start of the war. Russian soldiers were cursed by having too many foolish and proud commanders - a lot of them 'princes' with royal blood in their veins. It was small wonder that Russian soldiers formed the backbone of the Revolution which swept the Czar, the Russian Emperor, from power and took them out of the war in 1917.

TURKEY was known as 'the sick man' of Europe in 1914. By then the once-mighty Turkish Empire had already lost control of Greece, Serbia and Bulgaria. As a result of the war it lost control of the entire Arab world.

The Allies tried to invade Turkey via the peninsular of Gallipoli in 1915, but the turks were brave soldiers and beat them off with heavy losses. Later in the war, the Turks lost to the British army and its Arab allies who fought northwards from their bases in Arabia and Egypt. The British forces were led by General Allenby and supported by the hero, Lawrence of Arabia, who wore Arab dress and helped the Arab fighters.

Turkey lost nearly a million men during the war - a higher percentage of its army than any other country, including France and Germany.

Answers to Quiz Questions

Order your starters, page 24

1-bca. You can't demolish an entire country!
2-acb. Miners had nothing to do with it.
3-bca. A new moustache every day is impossible!

War fever, page 33

1-b. In August 1914 the bombing hadn't started.
2-c. Britain had a small army and no conscription.
3-b. 'Conchie' meant 'conscientious objector'.
4-b. Aliens in Britain were sent to internment camps.

Air slips, page 78

1. Parachutes weren't allowed until the end of the war.
2. Jet planes hadn't been invented yet.
3. Bombing of palaces was forbidden by the Kaiser.

A domestic scene, page 94

By 1917, it was forbidden to feed bread to dogs in Britain.

Fashion victim, page 103

1. Long hair, long skirts and no make-up were normal before the War.
2. Shorter hair, shorter skirts, make-up and smoking in public became acceptable during the War.

INDEX

NOW READ ON

This book gives an overview of the First World War. Here are a couple of other books, in case you want to read about the period in more detail. You should be able to find them in your local library.

GROWING UP IN THE FIRST WORLD WAR
By Renée Huggett (Batsford 1985) Although the focus is on children, this book is about far more than that. It paints an excellent picture of what life was like at the time of the Great War, both in Britain and further afield. It has a great many excellent photos which help bring the subject to life.

THE LAST CZAR
By WHC Smith (Wayland 1973) Czar Nicholas II and all his family were murdered by the Bolsheviks in Russia in 1917 (see page 108), at the start of the Russian Revolution. That Revolution, born out of the horror of the First World War, lead to the Cold War which has dominated recent history. This book tells the story of what went wrong.

ABOUT THE AUTHOR

Bob Fowke is a well-known author of children's books. With various friends and colleagues, he has created many unusual and entertaining works on all manner of subjects.

There's always more to his books than meets the eye - look at all the entries in the index of this one!

What They Don't Tell You About...
ORDER FORM

0 340 71330 5	ART	£3.99
0 340 63622 X	QUEEN VICTORIA	£3.99
0 340 63621 1	HENRY VIII	£3.99
0 340 69349 5	LIVING THINGS	£3.99
0 340 67093 2	SHAKESPEARE	£3.99
0 340 69350 9	STORY OF SCIENCE	£3.99
0 340 65614 X	ANCIENT EGYPTIANS	£3.99
0 340 65613 1	ELIZABETH I	£3.99
0 340 68611 1	VIKINGS	£3.99
0 340 68612 X	WORLD WAR II	£3.99
0 340 70922 7	ROMANS	£3.99
0 340 70921 9	ANGLO SAXONS	£3.99
0 340 71329 1	PLANET EARTH	£3.99
0 340 71328 3	ANCIENT GREEKS	£3.99
0 340 68995 1	STORY OF MUSIC	£3.99
0 340 73611 9	OLYMPICS	£3.99

All Hodder Children's books are available at your local bookshop or newsagent, or can be ordered direct from the publisher. Just write to the address below. Prices and availability subject to change without notice.

Hodder Children's Books, Cash Sales Department, Bookpoint, 39 Milton Park, Abingdon, Oxon, OX14 4TD, UK.
Email address: orders@bookpoint.co.uk

Please enclose a cheque or postal order made payable to Bookpoint Ltd to the value of the cover price and allow the following for postage and packing:
UK & BFPO - £1.00 for the first book, 50p for the second book, and 30p for each additional book ordered, up to a maximum charge of £3.00.
OVERSEAS & EIRE - £2.00 for the first book, £1.00 for the second book, and 50p for each additional book.

If you have a credit card you may order by telephone - (01235) 400414 (lines open 9 am - 6 pm, Monday to Saturday; 24 hour message answering service). Alternatively you can send a fax on 01235 400454.